# Diabetic Diet Made Easy

## 1500 Days of Wholesome Diabetic Dishes with 4-Week Meal Plans to Nourish Your Vitality | Full Color Edition

### Eugenia J. Cox

**Editor:** AALIYAH LYONS

**Interior Design:** BROOKE WHITE

**Cover Art:** DANIELLE REES

**Food stylist:** Sienna Adams

# Table Of Contents

# Introduction

*In the culinary realm of health and vitality, where flavor meets function, "Diabetic Diet Made Easy" stands as a beacon of empowerment and culinary delight. This book is not just a collection of recipes; it's a journey into the heart of mindful eating, designed to revolutionize the way we approach diabetes management through the joy of delicious, nourishing meals.*

*Imagine a world where every bite isn't just a source of sustenance but a symphony of flavors that nourish both the body and the soul. This cookbook is a passport to that world, where the constraints of a diabetic diet are transformed into an opportunity for culinary creativity. No longer are restrictions a hindrance; they become the catalyst for a gastronomic adventure that celebrates wholesome ingredients, vibrant spices, and the artistry of balanced cooking.*

*"Diabetic Diet Made Easy" is not about deprivation or sacrifice. It's a celebration of food as medicine, where each recipe is a step towards fostering a harmonious relationship between taste and well-being. From the sizzle of a sauté pan to the aroma of freshly chopped herbs, every page invites you to embrace the joy of cooking, demonstrating that managing diabetes can be a delectable and gratifying experience.*

*As you navigate through these pages, you'll discover more than just recipes – you'll find a roadmap to a lifestyle that harmonizes mindful eating with the demands of diabetes. Whether you're a seasoned chef or a novice in the kitchen, this book promises an exciting voyage, offering you the tools and inspiration to make every meal a masterpiece of healthful indulgence.*

*So, let the adventure begin. Say goodbye to bland and hello to a world where "Diabetic Diet Made Easy" is not just a book but a companion on your journey to rediscovering the sheer joy of eating well, living well, and thriving with diabetes.*

# Chapter 1

## Understanding Diabetes

# Types of Diabetes

Delving into the intricacies of diabetes reveals a nuanced landscape with distinct types, each presenting unique features and management challenges. This exploration aims to shed light on the diverse nature of diabetes, equipping individuals with a deeper understanding to make informed choices on their health journey.

## TYPE 1 DIABETES: DECIPHERING THE AUTOIMMUNE PUZZLE

At the core of Type 1 diabetes lies an intricate dance between genetics and the immune system. This type stands out as an autoimmune condition, where the body mistakenly attacks and annihilates the insulin-producing beta cells in the pancreas. This unrelenting assault results in a lifelong reliance on external insulin. Typically surfacing in childhood or adolescence, early detection is critical, with signs like excessive thirst, frequent urination, and unexplained weight loss serving as red flags.

## TYPE 2 DIABETES: LIFESTYLE FACTORS AND GENETIC THREADS

The most prevalent global variant, Type 2 diabetes, is often intricately woven with lifestyle choices and genetic predisposition. Its gradual development sees the body either resisting insulin's effects or failing to produce enough, leading to elevated glucose levels. Obesity, sedentary habits, and poor dietary decisions significantly contribute to its onset. Despite these factors, genetics play a pivotal role, emphasizing the need for personalized approaches to management. Lifestyle adjustments, oral medications, and insulin therapy often form part of the arsenal against Type 2 diabetes.

## GESTATIONAL DIABETES: NAVIGATING THE COMPLEXITIES OF PREGNANCY

A transient yet impactful type, gestational diabetes manifests during pregnancy, posing risks to both mother and fetus. Hormonal shifts compromise insulin sensitivity, resulting in heightened blood sugar levels. Although gestational diabetes typically resolves postpartum, it serves as a warning sign for increased Type 2 diabetes risk. Vigilant monitoring, dietary tweaks, and sometimes insulin therapy are crucial for ensuring a healthy pregnancy and preventing complications.

## LADA (LATENT AUTOIMMUNE DIABETES IN ADULTS): UNRAVELING THE GRADUAL ONSET ENIGMA

Occupying a distinctive niche, LADA shares characteristics with both Type 1 and Type 2 diabetes. Often initially misdiagnosed as Type 2 diabetes due to its onset in adulthood, LADA is an autoimmune condition featuring a slow decline in beta cell function. Initially responsive to oral medications, LADA eventually necessitates insulin as the autoimmune process progresses.

## MONOGENIC DIABETES: UNTANGLING THE GENETIC WEB

Unveiling the genetic complexity of diabetes, monogenic diabetes results from a single gene mutation, setting it apart from more common polygenic forms. Typically diagnosed in childhood or adolescence, monogenic diabetes necessitates precise treatment strategies based on genetic insights, distinguishing it from its more prevalent counterparts.

## Setting the Foundation

In the intricate tapestry of diabetes management, understanding and mastering nutritional basics stand as fundamental pillars. This exploration into the nutritional foundations aims to decode the complexities surrounding carbohydrates, proteins, and fats – key elements that wield significant influence over blood glucose levels and overall well-being.

### CARBOHYDRATES DECODED:
#### Identifying Healthy Carbohydrate Sources:

Carbohydrates are a primary energy source, but not all carbs are created equal. Mindful selection of carbohydrates can play a pivotal role in glycemic control. Opting for complex carbohydrates found in whole grains, legumes, and vegetables provides a sustained release of energy, helping to avoid sharp spikes in blood sugar levels. These nutrient-dense sources also contribute essential vitamins, minerals, and fiber, promoting overall health.

Awareness and education empower individuals to discern between simple and complex carbohydrates. Minimizing the intake of refined sugars and processed foods, which often lead to rapid blood glucose elevation, becomes a cornerstone in managing diabetes effectively. Instead, focusing on nutrient-rich, whole food sources establishes a foundation for stable and controlled blood sugar levels.

### GLYCEMIC INDEX AWARENESS:

The glycemic index (GI) is a valuable tool in navigating the carbohydrate landscape. It measures how quickly a particular food raises blood sugar levels. Low-GI foods release glucose more slowly, offering a gradual and sustained energy release. Incorporating low-GI foods, such as quinoa, legumes, and non-starchy vegetables, helps in managing post-meal blood sugar spikes.

However, it's essential to note that the glycemic index is not the sole determinant of a food's healthfulness. The overall nutritional composition and individual response to specific foods should be considered. Balancing low-GI choices with other nutrient-dense foods creates a comprehensive approach to carbohydrate management.

### BALANCING PROTEINS AND FATS:
#### Lean Proteins for Sustained Energy:

Proteins play a crucial role in maintaining stable blood sugar levels and promoting satiety. Lean protein sources, including poultry, fish, tofu, and legumes, offer a wealth of nutrients without excessive saturated fats. Integrating these proteins into meals helps in stabilizing energy levels and supporting muscle health, vital for overall metabolic well-being.

The key lies in moderation and variety, ensuring a diverse array of amino acids and nutrients. Balancing protein intake throughout the day provides a sustained release of energy, complementing the management of carbohydrates for individuals with diabetes.

### HEALTHY FATS AND THEIR ROLE IN DIABETES:

Dispelling the myth that all fats are detrimental, embracing healthy fats is paramount in diabetes management. Sources like avocados, nuts, seeds, and olive oil contribute monounsaturated and polyunsaturated fats, which can improve insulin sensitivity. These fats also aid in nutrient absorption, particularly fat-soluble vitamins like A, D, E, and K.

Omega-3 fatty acids, found in fatty fish like salmon and flaxseeds, showcase anti-inflammatory properties, potentially benefiting individuals with diabetes who may face heightened inflammation. However, portion control remains crucial, as fats are calorie-dense.

## Frequently Asked Questions

**Q1:** What is extreme blood sugar control in diabetes?

**A1:** Extreme blood sugar control refers to the strict management of blood glucose levels in individuals with diabetes. It involves maintaining blood sugar within a very narrow range, often lower than the conventional target levels. This approach aims to minimize fluctuations and keep glucose levels as close to normal as possible to prevent complications associated with diabetes.

**Q2:** Is extreme blood sugar control suitable for everyone with diabetes?

**A2:** Extreme blood sugar control may not be suitable for everyone. Factors such as age, overall health, and the presence of other medical conditions play a crucial role. It is essential to consult with a healthcare professional to determine an individualized approach to blood sugar management based on the specific needs and circumstances of the person with diabetes.

**Q3:** What are the potential benefits of extreme blood sugar control?

**A3:** The potential benefits of extreme blood sugar control include a reduced risk of diabetes-related complications such as cardiovascular diseases, kidney problems, and nerve damage. Tight control may also contribute to better overall health and improved quality of life for individuals with diabetes.

**Q4:** Are there risks associated with extreme blood sugar control?

**A4:** Yes, extreme blood sugar control comes with potential risks. It may increase the likelihood of hypoglycemia (low blood sugar), which can be dangerous and lead to symptoms such as dizziness, confusion, and, in severe cases, loss of consciousness. Additionally, maintaining extremely low blood sugar levels for an extended period may pose a risk of nutrient deficiencies and other adverse effects.

**Q5:** How can extreme blood sugar control impact daily life?

**A5:** Extreme blood sugar control can significantly impact daily life. It may require meticulous monitoring of dietary choices, physical activity, and medication adherence. The potential for frequent adjustments to insulin or other medications may also necessitate a structured routine to maintain tight control.

**Q6:** What role does diet play in extreme blood sugar control?

**A6:** Diet plays a pivotal role in extreme blood sugar control. Individuals may need to closely monitor carbohydrate intake, choose low-glycemic foods, and maintain a well-balanced diet to avoid drastic fluctuations in blood sugar levels.

**Q7:** How does physical activity contribute to extreme blood sugar control?

**A7:** Regular physical activity is crucial for individuals aiming for extreme blood sugar control. Exercise helps improve insulin sensitivity, allowing better regulation of blood sugar levels. However, it requires careful planning to prevent hypoglycemia during or after physical activity.

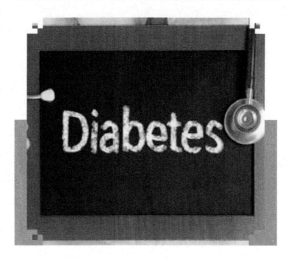

**Q8:** What are some recommended non-starchy vegetables for individuals with diabetes?

**A8:** Non-starchy vegetables like broccoli, spinach, bell peppers, and cauliflower are rich in fiber, vitamins, and minerals. They provide essential nutrients without significantly impacting blood sugar levels.

**Q9:** How can the cookbook incorporate whole grains beneficial for diabetes?

**A9:** The cookbook can feature whole grains like quinoa, brown rice, and oats in recipes. These grains offer fiber, promoting satiety and steady blood sugar levels.

**Q10:** What are examples of lean proteins suitable for a diabetic diet?

**A10:** Lean proteins such as skinless poultry, fish, tofu, and legumes can be featured in recipes. These sources help regulate blood sugar levels and support overall health.

**Q11:** What healthy fats can the cookbook include to enhance heart health in diabetes?

**A11:** The cookbook can incorporate healthy fats like avocados, nuts, and olive oil. These fats contribute to heart health without adversely affecting blood sugar levels.

**Q12:** How can the cookbook offer alternatives to refined sugars for sweet cravings?

**A12:** The cookbook can suggest sweeteners like stevia or monk fruit and cinnamon to satisfy cravings without causing blood sugar spikes.

**Q13:** What snacks does the cookbook recommend for stable blood sugar between meals?

**A13:** The cookbook can feature snacks like Greek yogurt with berries, raw vegetables with hummus, or a handful of nuts. These options provide a balance of nutrients and help maintain stable blood sugar levels.

In the rich tapestry of "Diabetic Diet Made Easy," the culmination of knowledge, culinary creativity, and a mindful approach to eating converges to redefine the landscape of diabetes management. From decoding the complexities of diabetes types to establishing a robust nutritional foundation. It serves as a guiding compass for individuals seeking not just nourishment but a holistic lifestyle transformation.

Embracing the principles of mindful eating, the cookbook navigates through the intricacies of extreme blood sugar control.

As the pages unfold, the cookbook beckons individuals to savor the joy of cooking, celebrating not only the artistry of well-balanced meals but also the empowerment that comes with informed choices. In its essence, this cookbook is not merely a collection of recipes; it is a companion on the path to rediscovering the joy of eating well, living well, and thriving with diabetes.

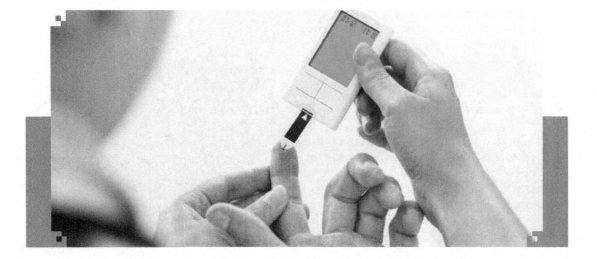

# Chapter 2

## 4-Week Meal Plan

## Week 1

### DAY 1:

- Breakfast: Coconut Pancakes
- Lunch: Juicy Turkey Burgers
- Snack: Cauliflower Hummus
- Dinner: Dry-Rubbed Sirloin

**TOTAL FOR THE DAY:**
Calories: 843; Fat: 50.1g; Carbs: 27.1g; Protein: 67.1g; Fiber: 8.1g

### DAY 2:

- Breakfast: Coconut Pancakes
- Lunch: Juicy Turkey Burgers
- Snack: Cauliflower Hummus
- Dinner: Dry-Rubbed Sirloin

**TOTAL FOR THE DAY:**
Calories: 843; Fat: 50.1g; Carbs: 27.1g; Protein: 67.1g; Fiber: 8.1g

### DAY 3:

- Breakfast: Coconut Pancakes
- Lunch: Juicy Turkey Burgers
- Snack: Cauliflower Hummus
- Dinner: Dry-Rubbed Sirloin

**TOTAL FOR THE DAY:**
Calories: 843; Fat: 50.1g; Carbs: 27.1g; Protein: 67.1g; Fiber: 8.1g

### DAY 4:

- Breakfast: Crispy Breakfast Pita with Egg
- Lunch: Dry-Rubbed Sirloin
- Snack: Cauliflower Hummus
- Dinner: Juicy Turkey Burgers

**TOTAL FOR THE DAY:**
Calories: 823; Fat: 46.1g; Carbs: 37.1g; Protein: 66.1g; Fiber: 6.1g

### DAY 5:

- Breakfast: Crispy Breakfast Pita with Egg
- Lunch: Dry-Rubbed Sirloin
- Snack: Cauliflower Hummus
- Dinner: Dry-Rubbed Sirloin

**TOTAL FOR THE DAY:**
Calories: 654; Fat: 38.1g; Carbs: 25.1g; Protein: 53.1g; Fiber: 5.1g

## Week 2

### DAY 1:

- Breakfast: Veggie Hash
- Lunch: Chicken Leg Roast
- Snack: Crunchy Apple Fries
- Dinner: Herbed Spring Peas

**TOTAL FOR THE DAY:**
Calories: 682; Fat: 29g; Carbs: 63.8g; Protein: 39g; Fiber: 13g

### DAY 2:

- Breakfast: Veggie Hash
- Lunch: Chicken Leg Roast
- Snack: Crunchy Apple Fries
- Dinner: Herbed Spring Peas

**TOTAL FOR THE DAY:**
Calories: 682; Fat: 29g; Carbs: 63.8g; Protein: 39g; Fiber: 13g

### DAY 3:

- Breakfast: Veggie Hash
- Lunch: Chicken Leg Roast
- Snack: Crunchy Apple Fries
- Dinner: Herbed Spring Peas

**TOTAL FOR THE DAY:**
Calories: 682; Fat: 29g; Carbs: 63.8g; Protein: 39g; Fiber: 13g

**DAY 4:**

- Breakfast: Veggie Hash
- Lunch: Herbed Spring Peas
- Snack: Crunchy Apple Fries
- Dinner: Chicken Leg Roast

**TOTAL FOR THE DAY:**
Calories: 682; Fat: 29g; Carbs: 63.8g; Protein: 39g; Fiber: 13g

**DAY 5:**

- Breakfast: Veggie Hash
- Lunch: Herbed Spring Peas
- Snack: Crunchy Apple Fries
- Dinner: Chicken Leg Roast

**TOTAL FOR THE DAY:**
Calories: 682; Fat: 29g; Carbs: 63.8g; Protein: 39g; Fiber: 13g

# Week 3

**DAY 1:**

- Breakfast: Pumpkin Apple Waffles
- Lunch: Honey Garlic Chicken
- Snack: Oatmeal Peanut Butter Bars
- Dinner: Blackened Catfish

**TOTAL FOR THE DAY:**
Calories: 597; Fat: 25g; Carbs: 61g; Protein: 35g; Fiber: 9g

**DAY 2:**

- Breakfast: Pumpkin Apple Waffles
- Lunch: Honey Garlic Chicken

- Snack: Oatmeal Peanut Butter Bars
- Dinner: Blackened Catfish

**TOTAL FOR THE DAY:**
Calories: 597; Fat: 25g; Carbs: 61g; Protein: 35g; Fiber: 9g

**DAY 3:**

- Breakfast: Pumpkin Apple Waffles
- Lunch: Honey Garlic Chicken
- Snack: Oatmeal Peanut Butter Bars
- Dinner: Blackened Catfish

**TOTAL FOR THE DAY:**
Calories: 597; Fat: 25g; Carbs: 61g; Protein: 35g; Fiber: 9g

**DAY 4:**

- Breakfast: Pumpkin Apple Waffles
- Lunch: Honey Garlic Chicken
- Snack: Oatmeal Peanut Butter Bars
- Dinner: Blackened Catfish

**TOTAL FOR THE DAY:**
Calories: 597; Fat: 25g; Carbs: 61g; Protein: 35g; Fiber: 9g

**DAY 5:**

- Breakfast: Pumpkin Apple Waffles
- Lunch: Honey Garlic Chicken
- Snack: Oatmeal Peanut Butter Bars
- Dinner: Honey Garlic Chicken

**TOTAL FOR THE DAY:**
Calories: 470; Fat: 14g; Carbs: 68g; Protein: 23g; Fiber: 9g

# Week 4

**DAY 1:**
- Breakfast: Hawaiian Breakfast Bake

- Lunch: Beef Burrito Bowl
- Snack: Spiced Rice Pudding
- Dinner: Roasted Delicata Squash

**TOTAL FOR THE DAY:**

Calories: 885; Fat: 32g; Carbs: 92g; Protein: 61g; Fiber: 11g

## DAY 2:

- Breakfast: Hawaiian Breakfast Bake
- Lunch: Beef Burrito Bowl
- Snack: Spiced Rice Pudding
- Dinner: Roasted Delicata Squash

**TOTAL FOR THE DAY:**

Calories: 885; Fat: 32g; Carbs: 92g; Protein: 61g; Fiber: 11g

## DAY 3:

- Breakfast: Hawaiian Breakfast Bake
- Lunch: Beef Burrito Bowl
- Snack: Spiced Rice Pudding
- Dinner: Roasted Delicata Squash

**TOTAL FOR THE DAY:**

Calories: 885; Fat: 32g; Carbs: 92g; Protein: 61g; Fiber: 11g

## DAY 4:

- Breakfast: Hawaiian Breakfast Bake
- Lunch: BBQ Chicken & Noodles
- Snack: Spiced Rice Pudding
- Dinner: BBQ Chicken & Noodles

**TOTAL FOR THE DAY:**

Calories: 1117; Fat: 36g; Carbs: 102g; Protein: 93g; Fiber: 9g

## DAY 5:

- Breakfast: Hawaiian Breakfast Bake
- Lunch: BBQ Chicken & Noodles
- Snack: Spiced Rice Pudding
- Dinner: BBQ Chicken & Noodles

**TOTAL FOR THE DAY:**

Calories: 1117; Fat: 36g; Carbs: 102g; Protein: 93g; Fiber: 9g

# Chapter 3

## Morning Pleasures

## Veggie Hash

**Prep time: 15 minutes | Cook time: 30 minutes | Serves 6 to 8**

- 2 tablespoons extra-virgin olive oil
- 1 small yellow onion, finely chopped
- 2 garlic cloves, minced
- ¼ cup Vegetable Broth
- 4 russet potatoes, cut into 1-inch cubes
- 2 cups okra, cut into 1-inch rounds

1. In a large cast iron skillet, heat the olive oil over medium-low heat.
2. Add the onion and garlic and cook for 3 to 5 minutes, or until translucent.
3. Add the broth, Creole seasoning covered, for 15 minutes.
4. Add the bell pepper, zucchini, summer squash, and okra. Cook,for 7 to 10 minutes, or until tender.
5. Serve with the Breakfast Casserole and spring greens of your choice for a weekend brunch.

**PER SERVING:**
Calories: 175 | Total Fat: 5g | Cholesterol: 0mg | Sodium: 76mg | Total Carbohydrates: 30g | Sugar: 5g | Fiber: 6g | Protein: 4g

## Coconut Pancakes

**Prep time: 5 minutes | Cook time: 15 to 20 minutes | Serves 4**

- ½ cup coconut flour
- 1 teaspoon baking powder
- ½ teaspoon ground cinnamon
- 8 large eggs
- ⅓ cup unsweetened almond milk
- 1 teaspoon vanilla extract

1. Heat a large skillet over medium-low heat.
2. In a large bowl, whisk together the flour, baking powder, cinnamon, and salt. Set aside.
3. In a medium bowl, whisk together the eggs, almond milk, oil, and vanilla. Pour the wet mixture into the dry ingredients and stir until combined.
4. Pour ⅓ cup of the batter onto the skillet for each pancake.about 7 minutes, then flip and cook for 1 minute more.

**PER SERVING**
Calories: 270 | Total Fat: 18g | Protein: 14g | Carbohydrates: 10g | Sugars: 2g | Fiber: 5g | Sodium: 325mg

## Crispy Breakfast Pita with Egg

**Prep time: 5 minutes | Cook time: 15 minutes | Serves 2**

- 1 (6-inch) whole-grain pita bread
- 3 teaspoons extra-virgin olive oil, divided
- 2 eggs
- 2 Canadian bacon slices
- juice of ½ lemon
- freshly ground black pepper

1. Heat a large skillet over medium heat. Cut the pita bread in half and brush. Cook for 2 to 3 minutes on each side, then remove from the skillet.
2. In the same skillet, heat 1 teaspoon of oil over medium heat.cook until the eggs are set, 2 to 3 minutes. Remove from the skillet.
3. Top each pita half with half of the microgreens, 1 piece of bacon, 1 egg, and 1 tablespoon of goat cheese. Season with pepper and serve.

**PER SERVING**

Calories: 250 | Total Fat: 14g | Protein: 13g | Carbohydrates: 20g | Sugars: 1g | Fiber: 3g | Sodium: 398mg

## Pumpkin Apple Waffles

**Prep time 10 minutes | Cook time: 20 minutes | Serves 6**

- 2¼ cups whole-wheat pastry flour
- 2 tablespoons granulated sweetener
- 1 tablespoon baking powder
- 1 teaspoon ground cinnamon
- 1¼ cups pure pumpkin purée
- melted coconut oil, for cooking

1. In a large bowl, stir together the flour, sweetener, baking powder, cinnamon, and nutmeg.
2. In a small bowl, whisk together the eggs and pumpkin.
3. Stir the apple into the batter.
4. Cook the waffles according to the waffle maker manufacturer's directions, brushing your waffle iron with melted coconut oil, until all the batter is gone.
5. Serve.

**PER SERVING**

Calories: 231 | Total Fat: 4g | Cholesterol: 141mg | Sodium: 51mg | Total Carbohydrates: 40g | Sugar: 5g | Fiber: 7g | Protein: 11g

## Open-Faced Egg Salad Sandwiches

**Prep time: 10 minutes | Cook time: none | Serves 4**

- 8 large hardboiled eggs
- 3 tablespoons plain low-fat Greek yogurt
- 1 tablespoon mustard
- ½ teaspoon freshly ground black pepper
- 1 teaspoon chopped fresh chives
- 4 slices 100% whole-wheat bread
- 2 cups fresh spinach, loosely packed

1. Peel the eggs and cut them in half.
2. In a large bowl, mash the eggs with a fork, leaving chunks.
3. Add the yogurt, mustard, pepper, and chives, and mix.
4. For each portion, layer 1 slice of bread with one-quarter of the egg salad and spinach.

### PER SERVING

Calories: 277 | Total Fat: 12g | Protein: 20g | Carbohydrates: 23g | Sugars: 3g | Fiber: 3g | Sodium: 364mg

## Apple Cinnamon Scones

**Prep time: 5 minutes| Cook time: 25 minutes| Serves 16**

- 2 large eggs
- 1 apple, diced
- ¼ cup + ½ tbsp. margarine
- 3 cups almond flour
- 1/3 cup + 2 tsp Splenda
- 1 tsp vanilla

1. Heat oven to 325 degrees. Line a large baking sheet with parchment paper.
2. In a large bowl, whisk flour, 1/3 cup Splenda, baking powder, 1 ½ teaspoons cinnamon, and salt together. Stir in apple.
3. Add the eggs, ¼ cup melted margarine, cream, and vanilla.
4. Bake 20-25 minutes, or until golden brown and firm to the touch.

### PER SERVING:

Calories: 176 |Total Carbs: 12g |Net Carbs: 9g |Protein: 5g |Fat: 12g |Sugar: 8g |Fiber: 3g

## Vanilla Steel-Cut Oatmeal

**Prep time: 5 minutes | Cook time: 40 minutes | Serves 4**

- 4 cups water
- pinch sea salt
- 1 cup steel-cut oats
- ¾ cup skim milk
- 2 teaspoons pure vanilla extract

1. In a large pot over high heat, bring the water and salt to a boil.
2. Reduce the heat to low and stir in the oats.
3. Cook the oats for about 30 minutes to soften, stirring occasionally.
4. Stir in the milk and vanilla and cook until your desired consistency is reached, about 10 more minutes.
5. Remove the cereal from the heat. Serve topped with sunflower seeds, chopped peaches, fresh berries, sliced almonds, or flaxseeds.

**PER SERVING**

Calories: 186 | Total Fat: 0g | Cholesterol: 1mg | Sodium: 36mg | Total Carbohydrates: 30g | Sugar: 2g | Fiber: 5g | Protein: 9g

## Hawaiian Breakfast Bake

**Prep time: 10 minutes| Cook time: 20 minutes| Serves 6**

- 6 slice ham, sliced thin
- 6 eggs
- ¼ cup reduced fat cheddar cheese, grated
- 6 pineapple slices
- 2 tbsp. salsa
- ½ tsp seasoning blend, salt-free

1. Heat oven to 350 degrees.
2. Line 6 muffin cups, or ramekins with sliced ham. Layer with cheese, salsa, and pineapple.
3. Crack one egg into each cup, sprinkle with seasoning blend.
4. If using ramekins place them on a baking sheet, bake 20-25 minutes or until egg whites are completely set but yolks are still soft. Serve immediately.

**PER SERVING:**

Calories: 135 |Total Carbs: 5g |Net Carbs: 4g |Protein: 12g |Fat: 8g |Sugar: 3g |Fiber: 1g

## Herbed Chicken Meatball Wraps

**Prep time: 10 minutes | Cook time: 20 minutes | Serves 6 (2 wraps each)**

- 1 pound ground chicken
- 3 scallions, both white and green parts, finely chopped
- 2 garlic cloves, minced
- ½ teaspoon dried oregano
- Cucumber-Yogurt Dip

1. Preheat the oven to 400°F. Line a baking sheet with parchment paper.
2. In a large mixing bowl, combine the chicken, scallions, garlic, mint, oregano, and egg. Stir well.
3. Bake for 10 minutes, flip with a spatula, and continue baking for an additional 10 minutes until the meatballs are cooked through.
4. In each lettuce leaf, place two meatballs and filling and serve with the dip.

**PER SERVING**

Calories: 220 | Total Fat: 12g | Protein: 23g | Carbohydrates: 6g | Sugars: 3g | Fiber: 2g | Sodium: 199mg

## Blueberry English Muffin Loaf

**Prep time: 15 minutes| Cook time: 1 hour| Serves 12**

- 6 eggs beaten
- ½ cup almond milk, unsweetened
- ½ cup blueberries
- ½ cup cashew butter
- ½ cup almond flour
- nonstick cooking spray

1. Heat oven to 350 degrees. Line a loaf pan with parchment paper and spray lightly with cooking spray.
2. In a small glass bowl, melt cashew butter and oil together in the microwave for 30 seconds. Stir until well combined.
3. Pour into the prepared pan and bake 45 minutes, or until it passes the toothpick test.
4. Cook 30 minutes, remove from pan and slice.

**PER SERVING:**

Calories: 162 |Total Carbs: 5g| Net Carbs: 4g| Protein: 6g |Fat: 14g| Sugar: 1g| Fiber: 1g

## Brussels Sprouts and Egg Scramble

**Prep time: 5 minutes | Cook time: 20 minutes|**
**Serves 4**

- Avocado oil cooking spray
- 4 slices low-sodium turkey bacon
- 20 Brussels sprouts, halved lengthwise
- 8 large eggs

1. Heat a large skillet over medium heat. and cook the bacon to your liking.
2. Divide the Brussels sprouts into 4 portions and Add 1 tablespoon of feta to each portion.

### PER SERVING

Calories: 253 | Total Fat: 15g | Protein: 21g | Carbohydrates: 10g | Sugars: 4g | Fiber: 4g | Sodium: 343mg

## Strawberry Kiwi Smoothies

**Prep time: 5 minutes| Cook time: 3 minutes|**
**Serves 4**

- 2 kiwi, peel & quarter
- 6 oz. strawberry yogurt
- 1 cup strawberries, frozen
- ½ cup skim milk
- 2 tbsp. honey

1. Place all Ingredients in a blender and process until smooth.
2. Pour into glasses and serve immediately.

### PER SERVING:

Calories: 120 |Total Carbs: 26g |Net Carbs: 24g |Protein: 3g |Fat: 1g |Sugar: 23g |Fiber: 2g

## Cottage Pancakes

**Prep time: 10 minutes | Cook time: 20 minutes | Serves 4**

- 2 cups low-fat cottage cheese
- 4 egg whites
- 2 eggs
- 1 tablespoon pure vanilla extract
- 1½ cups almond flour
- Nonstick cooking spray

1. Place the cottage cheese, egg whites, eggs, and vanilla in a blender and pulse to combine.
2. Add the almond flour to the blender and blend until smooth.
3. Spoon ¼ cup of batter per pancake, 4 at a time, into the skillet.until the bottoms are firm and golden, about 4 minutes.
4. Remove the pancakes to a plate and repeat with the remaining batter.
5. Serve with fresh fruit.

**PER SERVING**

Calories: 345 | Fat: 22.1g | Protein: 29.1g | Carbs: 11.1g | Fiber: 4.1g | Sugar: 5.1g | Sodium: 560mg

## Brussels Sprout Hash and Eggs

**Prep time: 15 minutes | Cook time: 15 minutes | Serves 4**

- 3 teaspoons extra-virgin olive oil, divided
- 1 pound Brussels sprouts, sliced
- 2 garlic cloves, thinly sliced
- ¼ teaspoon salt
- juice of 1 lemon
- 4 eggs

1. In a large skillet, heat 1½ teaspoons of oil over medium heat. Add the Brussels sprouts and toss. Cook, stirring regularly, for 6 to 8 minutes until browned and softened. Transfer to a serving dish.
2. In the same pan, heat the remaining 1½ teaspoons of oil over medium-high heat. continue cooking to desired doneness. Serve over the bed of hash.

**PER SERVING**

Calories: 158 | Total Fat: 9g | Protein: 10g | Carbohydrates: 12g | Sugars: 4g | Fiber: 4g | Sodium: 234mg

# Chapter 4

## Poultry Innovations

## Creamy Garlic Chicken with Broccoli

**Prep time: 5 minutes | Cook time: 15 minutes | Serves 4**

- ½ cup uncooked brown rice or quinoa
- 4 (4-ounce) boneless, skinless chicken breasts
- ¼ teaspoon salt
- ¼ teaspoon freshly ground black pepper
- 1 teaspoon garlic powder, divided
- 3 cups fresh or frozen broccoli florets
- 1 cup half-and-half

1. Cook the rice according to the package instructions.
2. Meanwhile, season both sides of the chicken breasts with the salt, pepper, and ½ teaspoon of garlic powder.
3. Divide the rice into four equal portions. Top each portion with 1 chicken breast and one-quarter of the broccoli and cream sauce.

### PER SERVING

Calories: 303 | Total Fat: 10g | Protein: 33g | Carbohydrates: 22g | Sugars: 4g | Fiber: 3g | Sodium: 271mg

## Juicy Turkey Burgers

**Prep time: 10 minutes | Cook time: 20 minutes | Serves 4**

- 1½ pounds lean ground turkey
- ½ cup bread crumbs
- ½ sweet onion, chopped
- 1 carrot, peeled, grated
- 1 teaspoon minced garlic
- 1 teaspoon chopped fresh thyme
- freshly ground black pepper
- nonstick cooking spray

1. In a large bowl, mix together the turkey, bread crumbs, onion, carrot, garlic, and thyme until very well mixed.
2. Season the mixture lightly with salt and pepper.
3. Shape the turkey mixture into 4 equal patties.
4. Serve the burgers plain or with your favorite toppings on a whole-wheat bun.

### PER SERVING

Calories: 317 | Total Fat: 15g | Cholesterol: 134mg | Sodium: 270mg | Total Carbohydrates: 12g | Sugar: 2g | Fiber: 1g | Protein: 32g

## Chicken Leg Roast

**Prep time: 10 minutes | Cook time: 35 minutes | Serves 6**

- 1 teaspoon ground paprika
- 1 teaspoon garlic powder
- ½ teaspoon ground cumin
- 6 chicken legs
- 1 teaspoon extra-virgin olive oil

1. Preheat the oven to 400 °F (205 °C).
2. In a bowl, cumin, paprika, garlic powder, salt, and cayenne pepper.
3. Add the chicken and cook for 9 minutes.
4. Place the skillet in the oven and chicken reaches a temperature of 165 °F (74 °C).
5. Take the chicken out of the oven and serve hot.

**PER SERVING**

Calories: 278 | Total Carbs: 0.8g | Net Carbs: 0.1g | Protein: 30g | Fat: 15g | Sugar: 0g | Fiber: 0g

## Honey Garlic Chicken

**Prep time: 5 minutes| Cook time: 6 hours| Serves 6**

- 6 chicken thighs
- 2 tbsp. sugar free ketchup
- 2 tbsp. honey
- 2 tbsp. lite soy sauce
- 3 cloves garlic, diced fine

1. Add everything, except chicken, to the crock pot. Stir to combine.
2. Lay chicken, skin side up, in a single layer. Cover and cook on low 6 hours, or high for 3 hours.
3. Place chicken in a baking dish and broil 2-3 minutes to caramelize the outside. Serve.

**PER SERVING:**

Calories: 57 |Total Carbs: 7g |Protein: 4g |Fat: 2g |Sugar: 6g |Fiber: 0g

## Turkey Stuffed Peppers

**Prep time: 10 minutes| Cook time: 55 minutes|**
**Serves 8**

- 1 lb. lean ground turkey
- 4 green bell peppers, halved and ribs and seeds removed
- 1 onion, diced
- 1 ½ cup mozzarella cheese
- 1 cup mushrooms, diced
- 3 cups spaghetti sauce
- 3 cloves garlic, diced fine

1. Heat the oil in a large skillet over med-high heat. Add the garlic, mushrooms, and onion.until turkey is cooked through, about 10 minutes.
2. Stir in the cauliflower, and cook, stirring frequently, 3-5 minutes. Stir to combine and remove from heat.
3. Heat oven to 350 degrees. Place bell peppers in a large baking dish, skin side down. Bake 40-45 minutes or the peppers are tender. Serve immediately.

**PER SERVING:**

Calories: 214 |Total Carbs: 14g |Net Carbs: 10g |Protein: 20g |Fat: 11g |Sugar: 9g |Fiber: 4g

## Cheesy Chicken & Spinach

**Prep time: 10 minutes| Cook time: 45 minutes|**
**Serves 6**

- 3 chicken breasts, boneless, skinless and halved lengthwise
- 6 oz. low fat cream cheese, soft
- 2 cup baby spinach
- 1 cup mozzarella cheese, grated
- 2 tbsp. olive oil, divided
- nonstick cooking spray

1. Heat oven to 350 degrees. Spray a 9x13-inch glass baking dish with cooking spray.
2. Lay chicken breast cutlets in baking dish. Drizzle 1 tablespoon oil over chicken. Sprinkle evenly with garlic and Italian seasoning. Spread cream cheese over the top of chicken.
3. Heat remaining tablespoon of oil in a small skillet over medium heat. Add spinach and cook.Place evenly over cream cheese layer. Sprinkle mozzarella over top.
4. Bake 35-40 minutes, or until chicken is cooked through. Serve.

**PER SERVING:**

Calories: 363 |Total Carbs: 3g |Protein: 31g |Fat: 25g |Sugar: 0g |Fiber: 0g

## Turkey Meatloaf Muffins

**Prep time: 10 minutes | Cook time: 35 minutes | Serves 12 (2 muffins each)**

- nonstick cooking spray
- ½ cup old-fashioned oats
- 1 pound lean ground turkey
- ½ cup finely chopped onion
- 1 red bell pepper, seeded and finely chopped
- 2 eggs
- 3 garlic cloves, minced
- 1 teaspoon salt
- ½ teaspoon freshly ground black pepper

1. Preheat the oven to 375°F. Lightly spray a 12-cup muffin tin.
2. In a blender, process the oats until they become flour.
3. Bake for 30 to 35 minutes until the muffins are cooked through.
4. Slide a knife along the outside of each cup and remove. Serve warm.

**PER SERVING**

Calories: 88 | Total Fat: 4g | Protein: 9g | Carbohydrates: 4g | Sugars: 1g | Fiber: 1g | Sodium: 203mg

## Cast Iron Hot Chicken

**Prep time: 10 minutes | Cook time: 40 minutes | Serves 4**

- 2 boneless, skinless chicken breasts
- Juice of 2 limes
- 2 garlic cloves, minced
- 1 medium yellow onion, chopped
- 1½ teaspoons cayenne pepper
- 1 teaspoon smoked paprika

1. Preheat the oven to 375°F.
2. In a shallow bowl, massage the chicken all over with the lime juice, garlic, onion, cayenne, and paprika.
3. In a cast iron skillet, place the chicken in one even layer.
4. Transfer the skillet to the oven and cook for 35 to 40 minutes, or until cooked through.
5. Remove the chicken from the oven, and let rest for 5 minutes.
6. Divide each breast into two portions. Serve with Not Slow-Cooked Collards.

**PER SERVING:**

Calories: 117 | Total Fat: 1g | Cholesterol: 49mg | Sodium: 59mg | Total Carbohydrates: 7g | Sugar: 2g | Fiber: 2g | Protein: 20g

## Turkey Taco

**Prep time: 10 minutes | Cook time: 20 minutes | Serves 4**

- 3 tablespoons extra-virgin olive oil
- 1 pound (454 g) ground turkey
- 1 onion, chopped
- 1 green bell pepper, seeded and chopped
- ½ teaspoon sea salt
- 1 small head cauliflower, grated
- 1 cup corn kernels
- ½ cup prepared salsa
- 1 cup shredded pepper Jack cheese

1. In a large non-stick skillet, heat over medium-high heat until the olive oil is shiny.
2. Add the turkey.
3. Mix with a spoon browned, about 5 minutes.
4. Add the onion, pepper, and salt.
5. Cook, stirring occasionally, for 4 to 5 minutes, until the vegetables are tender.
6. Reduce the heat to low, cover, and let the cheese melt for 2-3 minutes.

### PER SERVING

Calories: 449 | Total Carbs: 17g | Net Carbs: 12g | Protein: 30g | Fat: 30g | Sugar: 8.7g | Fiber: 4.1g

## Roasted Vegetable and Chicken Tortillas

**Prep time: 10 minutes | Cook time: 20 minutes | Serves 4**

- 1 red bell pepper, seeded and cut into 1-inch-wide strips
- ½ small eggplant, cut into ¼-inch-thick slices
- ½ small red onion, sliced
- 1 medium zucchini, cut lengthwise into strips
- 2 (8-ounce / 227-g) cooked chicken breasts, sliced

1. Preheat the oven to 400°F (205°C). Line a baking sheet with aluminum foil.
2. Combine the bell pepper, eggplant, red onion, zucchini.
3. Roast in the preheated oven for 20 minutes or until tender and charred.
4. Unfold the tortillas on a clean work surface, then divide the vegetables and chicken slices on the tortillas.
5. Wrap and serve immediately.

### PER SERVING

Calories: 483 | Fat: 25.0g | Protein: 20.0g | Carbs: 45.0g | Fiber: 3.0g | Sugar: 4.0g | Sodium: 730mg

## Ginger Citrus Chicken Thighs

**Prep time: 15 minutes | Cook time: 30 minutes | Serves 4**

- 4 chicken thighs, bone-in, skinless
- 1 tablespoon grated fresh ginger
- sea salt
- 1 tablespoon extra-virgin olive oil
- juice and zest of ½ lemon
- 2 tablespoons honey
- 1 tablespoon chopped fresh cilantro

1. Rub the chicken thighs with the ginger and season lightly with salt.
2. Place a large skillet over medium-high heat and add the oil.
3. Brown the chicken thighs, turning once, for about 10 minutes.
4. Braise until the chicken is cooked through, about 20 minutes, adding a couple of tablespoons of water if the pan is too dry.
5. Serve garnished with the cilantro.

**PER SERVING**

Calories: 114 | Total Fat: 5g | Cholesterol: 34mg | Sodium: 287mg | Total Carbohydrates: 9g | Sugar: 9g | Fiber: 0g | Protein: 9g

## Curried Chicken and Apples

**Prep time: 15 minutes | Cook time: 30 minutes | Serves 4**

- 1 pound (454 g) chicken breasts, boneless, skinless, cut in 1-inch cubes
- 2 tart apples, peel and slice
- 1 sweet onion, cut in half and slice
- 3 cloves garlic, diced
- 2 tablespoons sunflower oil
- ½ teaspoon turmeric
- ¼ teaspoon cayenne pepper

1. Heat oil in a large skillet over medium-high heat. Add chicken and onion, and cook until onion is tender. Add garlic and cook 1 more minute.
2. Add apples, water and seasonings and stir to combine. Bring to a boil. Reduce heat and simmer 12 to 15 minutes, or until chicken is cooked through, stirring occasionally.
3. Stir in tomatoes, jalapeno, and cilantro and serve.

**PER SERVING**

Calories: 372 | Fat: 16.0g | Protein: 34.2g | Carbs: 23.1g | Fiber: 5.0g | Sugar: 15.0g | Sodium: 705mg

# Chapter 5

## Pork, Lamb & Beef Gourmet

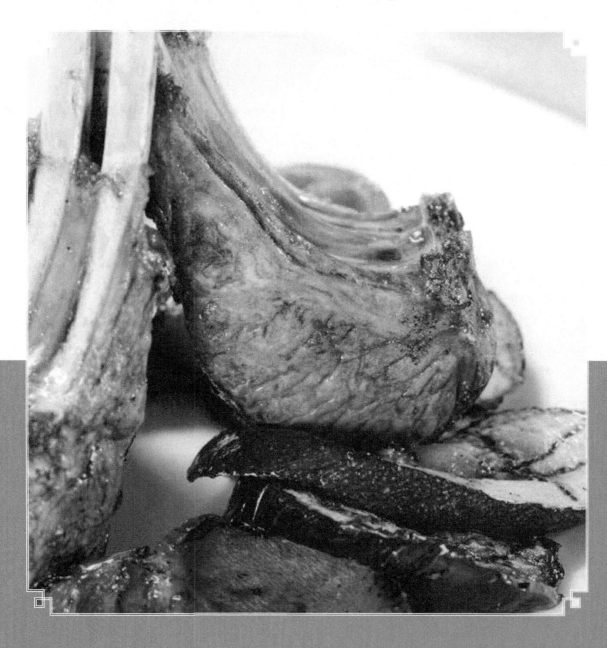

## One Pot Beef & Veggies

**Prep time: 15 minutes |Cook time: 8 hours| Serves 10**

- 3 lb. beef roast
- 1 lb. red potatoes, cubed
- ¼ lb. mushrooms
- 1 green bell pepper, diced
- 1 parsnip, diced
- ¾ tsp salt
- ¾ tsp oregano
- ¼ tsp pepper

1. Place the vegetables in a large crock pot. place on top of vegetables.
2. Combine broth, salt, oregano, and pepper, pour over meat.
3. Remove meat and vegetables to a serving platter, transfer to a small saucepan.
4. Place pan over medium heat and bring to a boil. Serve with roast.

**PER SERVING:**

Calories: 381 |Total Carbs: 28g |Net Carbs: 22g |Protein: 46g |Fat: 9g |Sugar: 12g |Fiber: 6g

## Garlic Butter Steak

**Prep time: 5 minutes| Cook time: 8 minutes| Serves 4**

- 1 lb. skirt steak
- 1/4 cup fresh parsley, diced, divided
- 5 tbsp. margarine
- 6 tsp garlic, diced fine
- 1 tbsp. olive oil
- salt and pepper for taste

1. Cut the steak into 4 pieces. Pat dry then season both sides with salt and pepper
2. Heat oil in a large, heavy skillet over med-high heat.Transfer to plate and cover with foil to keep warm.
3. Pour the garlic mixture into a bowl and season with salt to taste. Slice the steak against the grain and place on plates. Sprinkle parsley over steak then drizzle with garlic mixture. Serve immediately.

**PER SERVING:**

Calories: 365 |Total Carbs: 2g |Protein: 31g |Fat: 25g |Sugar: 0g |Fiber: 0g

## Cheesesteak Stuffed Peppers

**Prep time: 15 minutes |Cook time: 35 minutes |Serves 4**

- 4 slices low-salt deli roast beef, cut into 1/2-inch strips
- 4 slices mozzarella cheese, cut in half
- 2 large green bell peppers, slice in half
- 2 tsp garlic, diced fine
- ¼ tsp black pepper

1. Heat oven to 400 degrees. Place peppers, skin side down, in baking dish.
2. Remove from heat and stir in roast beef.
3. Place a piece of cheese inside each Cover with foil and bake 20 minutes.
4. Remove the foil and top each pepper with remaining cheese. Bake another 5 minutes, or until cheese is melted.

**PER SERVING:**

Calories: 191 |Total Carbs: 10g |Net Carbs: 8g |Protein: 12g |Fat: 12g |Sugar: 5g |Fiber: 2g

## Dry-Rubbed Sirloin

**Prep time: 5 minutes | Cook time: 15 minutes | Serves 6**

- 1⅛ pounds beef round sirloin tip
- 2 tablespoons Creole Seasoning
- 2 tomatoes

1. Preheat the oven to 375°F.
2. Massage the beef all over with the Creole seasoning.
3. Put the beef and tomatoes in a Dutch oven, cover, and transfer to the oven. Cook for 15 minutes, or until the juices run clear when you pierce the beef.
4. Remove the beef from the oven, and let rest for 15 minutes.
5. Carve and serve.

**PER SERVING:**

Calories: 148 | Total Fat: 7g | Cholesterol: 54mg | Sodium: 47mg | Total Carbohydrates: 0g | Sugar: 0g | Fiber: 0g | Protein: 19g

## Asian Beef Bowls

**Prep time: 15 minutes| Cook time: 15 minutes|**
**Serves 4**

- 1 lb. lean ground beef
- 1 bunch green onions, sliced
- ¼ cup fresh ginger, grated
- cauliflower rice
- 2 tbsp. light soy sauce
- 2 tsp sesame seeds

1.  Heat oil in a large, cast-iron skillet over high heat.starting to brown, about 5 minutes.
2.  Add beef, and cook, breaking up with a spatula, until no longer pink. About 8 minutes.
3.  Add remaining Ingredients and simmer 2-3 minutes, stirring frequently. Serve over hot cauliflower rice garnished with sesame seeds and reserved green onions.

**PER SERVING:**
Calories: 383 |Total Carbs: 24g |Net Carbs: 22g |Protein: 40g |Fat: 21g |Sugar: 11g |Fiber: 2g

## Mustard-Glazed Pork Chops

**Prep time: 5 minutes | Cook time: 25 minutes |**
**Serves 4**

- ¼ cup Dijon mustard
- 1 tablespoon pure maple syrup
- 2 tablespoons rice vinegar
- 4 bone-in, thin-cut pork chops

1.  Preheat the oven to 400°F.
2.  In a small saucepan, combine the mustard, maple syrup, and rice vinegar. Stir to mix and bring to a simmer over medium heat. Cook for about 2 minutes until just slightly thickened.
3.  In a baking dish, place the pork chops and spoon the sauce over them, flipping to coat.
4.  Bake, uncovered, for 18 to 22 minutes until the juices run clear.

**PER SERVING**
Calories: 257 | Total Fat: 7g | Protein: 39g | Carbohydrates: 7g | Sugars: 4g | Fiber: 0g | Sodium: 466mg

## Beef and Mushroom Cauliflower Wraps

**Prep time: 5 minutes | Cook time: 20 minutes | Serves 4**

- Avocado oil cooking spray
- ½ cup chopped white onion
- 1 cup chopped portobello mushrooms
- ½ teaspoon garlic powder
- 1 (10-ounce / 283-g) bag frozen cauliflower rice
- 12 iceberg lettuce leaves
- ¾ cup shredded Cheddar cheese

1. Heat a large skillet over medium heat. add the onion and mushrooms. Cook for 5 minutes.
2. Add the beef, garlic powder, and salt, stirring and breaking apart the meat as needed. Cook for 5 minutes.
3. For each portion, use three lettuce leaves. Spoon one-quarter of the filling onto the lettuce leaves, roll up the lettuce to close the wrap. Repeat with the remaining lettuce leaves and filling.

### PER SERVING
Calories: 290 | Fat: 15.1g | Protein: 31.1g | Carbs: 7.1g | Fiber: 3.1g | Sugar: 4.0g | Sodium: 265mg

## Steak with Peanut Sauce

**Prep time: 10 minutes | Cook time: 15 minutes | Serves 4**

- ⅓ cup light coconut milk
- 1 teaspoon curry powder
- 1 teaspoon coriander powder
- 1 teaspoon low-sodium soy sauce
- 1 ¼-lb. skirt steak
- Cooking spray
- ½ cup Asian peanut sauce

1. In a suitable bowl, whisk together the coconut milk, curry powder, coriander powder, and soy sauce.
2. Add the steak and turn to coat. Cover the bowl and refrigerate for at least 30 minutes.
3. Preheat the barbecue or coat a grill pan with cooking spray and place the steak over medium-high heat.
4. Slice the steak into 5-ounce pieces and serve each with 2 tablespoons of the Asian peanut sauce.

### PER SERVING
Calories: 361 | Fats: 22g | Net Carbs: 5g | Net Carbs: 1g | Proteins: 36g | Total Carbs: 8g | Sugars: 1g | Fiber: 5g

## Steak and Broccoli Bowls

**Prep time: 10 minutes | Cook time: 15 minutes | Serves 4**

- 2 tablespoons extra-virgin olive oil
- 1 pound (454 g) sirloin steak, cut into ¼-inch-thick strips
- 2 cups broccoli florets
- 1 teaspoon peeled and grated fresh ginger
- 2 tablespoons reduced-sodium soy sauce
- ¼ cup beef broth
- Pinch red pepper flakes

1. In a large skillet over medium-high heat, heat the olive oil until it shimmers. Add the beef. Cook, stirring, until it browns, 3 to 5 minutes. with a slotted spoon, remove the beef from the oil and set it aside on a plate.
2. Add the broccoli to the oil. Cook, stirring, until it is crisp-tender, about 4 minutes.
3. Add the soy sauce mixture to the skillet and cook, stirring, until everything warms through, about 3 minutes.

**PER SERVING**
Calories: 230 | Fat: 11.1g | Protein: 27.1g | Carbs: 4.9g | Fiber: 1.0g | Sugar: 3.0g | Sodium: 376mg

## Beef Goulash

**Prep time: 15 minutes | Cook time: 1 hour | Serves 6**

- 2 pounds (907 g) chuck steak, trim fat and cut into bite-sized pieces
- 3 onions, quartered
- 1 orange pepper, chopped
- 3 cups water
- 1 can tomatoes, chopped
- 1 cup low sodium beef broth
- 1 tablespoon paprika
- Salt and ground black pepper, to taste

1. Heat oil in a large soup pot over medium-high. Add steak and cook until browned, stirring frequently. Add onions and cook 5 minutes. Add garlic and cook another minute, stirring frequently.
2. Add remaining.Reduce heat to medium-low and simmer 45 to 50 minutes,Goulash is done when steak is tender. Stir well before serving.

**PER SERVING**
Calories: 412 | Fat: 15.0g | Protein: 53.1g | Carbs: 14.1g | Fiber: 3.0g | Sugar: 8.0g | Sodium: 159mg

# Chapter 6

## Fish & Seafood Bonanza

## Lemon Pepper Salmon

**Prep time: 5 minutes | Cook time: 20 minutes | Serves 4**

- Avocado oil cooking spray
- 20 Brussels sprouts, halved lengthwise
- 4 (4-ounce) skinless salmon fillets
- ½ teaspoon garlic powder
- ½ teaspoon freshly ground black pepper
- ¼ teaspoon salt
- 2 teaspoons freshly squeezed lemon juice

1. Heat a large skillet over medium-low heat. When hot,cut-side down in the skillet. Cover and cook for 5 minutes.
2. Meanwhile, season both sides of the salmon with the garlic powder, pepper, and salt.
3. Flip the Brussels sprouts, and move them to one side of the skillet.for 4 to 6 minutes.
4. Divide the Brussels sprouts into four equal portions and Sprinkle the lemon juice on top and serve.

**PER SERVING**

Calories: 193 | Total Fat: 7g | Protein: 25g | Carbohydrates: 10g | Sugars: 2g | Fiber: 4g | Sodium: 222mg

## Italian Steamed Mussels

**Prep time: 10 minutes| Cook time: 10 minutes| Serves 4**

- 2 lbs. mussels, cleaned
- 2 plum tomatoes, peeled, seeded and diced
- 1 cup onion, diced
- 2 tbsp. fresh parsley, diced
- 2 tbsp. fresh breadcrumbs
- ¼ teaspoon crushed red pepper flakes

1. Heat oil in a large sauce pot over medium heat.about 2-3 minutes. Add garlic and cook 1 minute more.
2. Stir in wine, tomatoes, and pepper flakes. Bring to a boil, stirring occasionally.Discard any mussels that do not open.
3. Once mussels open, transfer them to a serving bowl. Add bread crumbs to the sauce and continue to cook,Stir in parsley and pour evenly over mussels. Serve.

**PER SERVING:**

Calories: 340 |Total Carbs: 18g |Net Carbs: 16g |Protein: 29g |Fat: 16g |Sugar: 4g |Fiber: 2g

## Scallops and Asparagus Skillet

**Prep time: 10 minutes | Cook time: 15 minutes | Serves 4**

- 3 teaspoons extra-virgin olive oil, divided
- 1 pound asparagus
- 1 pound sea scallops
- ¼ cup dry white wine
- juice of 1 lemon
- 2 garlic cloves, minced
- ¼ teaspoon freshly ground black pepper

1. In a large skillet, heat 1½ teaspoons of oil over medium heat.
2. Add the asparagus and sauté for 5 to 6 minutes. Remove from the skillet and cover with aluminum foil to keep warm.
3. Return the asparagus and the cooked scallops to the skillet to coat with the sauce. Serve warm.

**PER SERVING**

Calories: 252 | Total Fat: 7g | Protein: 26g | Carbohydrates: 15g | Sugars: 3g | Fiber: 2g | Sodium: 493mg

## Tangy Orange Roughy

**Prep time: 5 minutes | Cook time: 15 minutes | Serves 4**

- 4 orange roughy filets
- ¼ cup fresh lemon juice
- ¼ cup reduced sodium soy sauce
- 1 tablespoon Splenda
- ½ teaspoon ginger
- ½ teaspoon lemon pepper
- Nonstick cooking spray

1. In a large Ziploc bag combine lemon juice, soy sauce, Splenda, and ginger. Add fish, seal, and turn to coat. Refrigerate 30 minutes.
2. Heat oven to 350°F (180°C). Spray a large baking sheet with cooking spray.
3. Place filets on prepared pan and sprinkle with lemon pepper. Bake 12 to 15 minutes, or until fish flakes easily with fork.

**PER SERVING**

Calories: 238 | Fat: 12.0g | Protein: 25.2g | Carbs: 4.1g | Fiber: 1.0g | Sugar: 4.0g | Sodium: 656mg

## Broiled Cod with Mango Salsa

**Prep time: 10 minutes | Cook time: 5 to 10 minutes | Serves 4**

Cod:

- 1 pound (454 g) cod, cut into 4 fillets, pin bones removed
- ¾ teaspoon sea salt, divided
- Mango Salsa:
- 1 mango, pitted, peeled, and cut into cubes
- 1 garlic clove, minced

1. Preheat the broiler to high.
2. Place the cod fillets on a rimmed baking Sprinkle with ½ teaspoon of the salt.
3. Meanwhile, make the mango salsa remaining salt in a small bowl.
4. Serve the cod warm topped with the mango salsa.

**PER SERVING**

Calories: 198 | Fat: 8.1g | Protein: 21.2g | Carbs: 13.2g | Fiber: 2.2g | saturated fat: 1g | Sodium: 355mg

## Cajun Flounder & Tomatoes

**Prep time: 10 minutes| Cook time: 15 minutes| Serves 4**

- 4 flounder fillets
- 2 ½ cups tomatoes, diced
- ¾ cup onion, diced
- ¾ cup green bell pepper, diced
- 2 cloves garlic, diced fine
- 1 tbsp. cajun seasoning
- 1 tsp olive oil

1. Heat oil in a large skillet over med-high heat. Add onion and garlic and cook 2 minutes, or until soft. Add tomatoes, peppers and spices, and cook 2-3 minutes until tomatoes soften.
2. Lay fish over top. Cover, reduce heat to medium and cook, 5-8 minutes, or until fish flakes easily with a fork. Transfer fish to serving plates and top with sauce.

**PER SERVING:**

Calories: 194 |Total Carbs: 8g |Net Carbs: 6g |Protein: 32g |Fat: 3g |Sugar: 5g |Fiber: 2g

## Herb-Crusted Halibut

**Prep time: 10 minutes | Cook time: 20 minutes | Serves 4**

- 4 (5-ounce) halibut fillets
- extra-virgin olive oil, for brushing
- ½ cup coarsely ground unsalted pistachios
- 1 tablespoon chopped fresh parsley
- 1 teaspoon chopped fresh thyme
- pinch freshly ground black pepper

1. Preheat the oven to 350°F.
2. Line a baking sheet with parchment paper.
3. Pat the halibut fillets dry with a paper towel and place them on the baking sheet.
4. Brush the halibut generously with olive oil.
5. Bake the halibut until it flakes when pressed with a fork, about 20 minutes.
6. Serve immediately.

**PER SERVING**

Calories: 262 | Total Fat: 11g | Cholesterol: 45mg | Sodium: 77mg | Total Carbohydrates: 4g | Sugar: 1g | Fiber: 2g | Protein: 32g

## Shrimp & Artichoke Skillet

**Prep time: 5 minutes| Cook time: 10 minutes| Serves 4**

- 1 ½ cups shrimp, peel & devein
- 2 shallots, diced
- 1 tbsp. margarine
- 2 12 oz. jars artichoke hearts, drain & rinse
- 2 cups white wine
- 2 cloves garlic, diced fine

1. Melt margarine in a large skillet over med-high heat. Add shallot and garlic and cook until they start to brown, stirring frequently.
2. Add artichokes and cook 5 minutes. Reduce heat and add wine. Cook 3 minutes, stirring occasionally.
3. Add the shrimp and cook just until they turn pink. Serve.

**PER SERVING:**

Calories: 487 |Total Carbs: 26g |Net Carbs: 17g |Protein: 64g |Fat: 5g |Sugar: 3g |Fiber: 9g

## Blackened Catfish

**Prep time: 15 minutes | Cook time: 20 minutes | Serves 4**

- ½ cup Blackened Rub
- 1 teaspoon dried oregano
- 1 teaspoon dried parsley
- ½ teaspoon cayenne pepper
- 4 (4-ounce) skinless catfish fillets
- 2 tablespoons sunflower seed oil

1. In a small bowl, mix the rub, oregano, parsley, and cayenne pepper together.
2. Dredge the catfish in the spice mixture, turning until well coated, and set aside to marinate for 10 minutes.
3. Heat a cast iron skillet over high heat for 2 to 3 minutes, or until smoking.
4. Pour the oil into the pan. cook for 5 to 7 minutes per side, or until opaque.
5. Serve.

**PER SERVING:**
Calories: 184 | Total Fat: 13g | Cholesterol: 45mg | Sodium: 60mg | Total Carbohydrates: 0g | Sugar: 0g | Fiber: 0g | Protein: 16g

## Crunchy Lemon Shrimp

**Prep time: 5 minutes| Cook time: 10 minutes| Serves 4**

- 1 lb. raw shrimp, peeled and deveined
- 2 tbsp. Italian parsley, roughly chopped
- 2 tbsp. lemon juice, divided
- ⅔ cup panko bread crumbs
- 2½ tbsp. olive oil, divided
- salt and pepper, to taste

1. Heat oven to 400 degrees.
2. Place the shrimp evenly in a baking dish Drizzle on 1 tablespoon lemon juice and 1 tablespoon of olive oil. Set aside.
3. In a medium bowl, combine parsley, remaining lemon juice, bread crumbs, Layer the panko mixture evenly on top of the shrimp.
4. Bake 8-10 minutes or until shrimp are cooked through and the panko is golden brown.

**PER SERVING:**
Calories: 283 |Total Carbs: 15g |Net Carbs: 14g |Protein: 28g |Fat: 12g |Sugar: 1g |Fiber: 1g

## Breaded Scallop Patties

**Prep time: 15 minutes | Cook time: 10 to 14 minutes | Serves 4**

- 4 medium egg whites
- 1 cup chickpea crumbs
- ½ cup fat-free milk
- ½ teaspoon ground cumin
- ¼ teaspoon freshly ground black pepper
- 3 cups frozen chopped scallops, thawed
- 1 small green bell pepper, finely chopped
- Juice of 2 limes

1. Preheat the oven to 350°F (180°C).
2. Whisk together the egg whites, chickpea crumbs, milk, cumin, and black pepper in a large bowl until well combined.
3. Bake in the preheated oven for 10 to 14 minutes until golden brown. Flip the patties halfway through the cooking time.
4. Serve drizzled with the lime juice.

**PER SERVING**

Calories: 338 | Fat: 0g | Protein: 50.2g | Carbs: 24.2g | Fiber: 6.2g | Sugar: 4.2g | Sodium: 465mg

## Panko Coconut Shrimp

**Prep time: 12 minutes | Cook time: 6 to 8 minutes | Serves 4**

- 2 egg whites
- 1 tablespoon water
- ½ cup whole-wheat panko bread crumbs
- ¼ cup unsweetened coconut flakes
- ½ teaspoon turmeric
- 1 pound large raw shrimp, peeled, deveined, and patted dry
- Nonstick cooking spray

1. Preheat the air fry to 400°F (205°C).
2. In a shallow dish, beat the egg whites and water until slightly foamy. Set aside.
3. Air fry for 6 to 8 minutes, flipping the shrimp once during cooking, or until the shrimp are golden brown and cooked through.
4. Let the shrimp cool for 5 minutes before serving.

**PER SERVING**

Calories: 181 | Fat: 4.2g | Protein: 27.8g | Carbs: 9.0g | Fiber: 2.3g | Sugar: 0.8g | Sodium: 227mg

# Chapter 7

## Delicious Vegetables and Salads

## Herbed Spring Peas

**Prep time: 10 minutes | Cook time: 15 minutes | Serves 6**

- 1 tablespoon unsalted non-hydrogenated plant-based butter
- ½ Vidalia onion, thinly sliced
- 1 cup Vegetable Broth or store-bought low-sodium vegetable broth
- 3 cups fresh shelled peas
- 1 tablespoon minced fresh tarragon

1. In a skillet, melt the butter over medium heat.
2. Add the onion and sauté for 2 to 3 minutes.
3. Add the peas and tarragonServe with Coastal Creole Shrimp.

**PER SERVING:**
Calories: 83 | Total Fat: 2g | Cholesterol: 0mg | Sodium: 50mg | Total Carbohydrates: 12g | Sugar: 5g | Fiber: 4g | Protein: 4g

## Greek Chickpea Salad

**Prep time: 5 minutes| Cook time: none | Serves 4**

- 2 cups diced cucumber
- 2 cups diced tomatoes
- 1½ cups canned low-sodium chickpeas, drained and rinsed
- ½ cup sliced red onion
- ¼ cup crumbled feta
- 8 pitted green olives, drained, rinsed, and halved
- ¾ cup Creamy Dill Dressing

1. In a large bowl, combine the cucumber, tomatoes, chickpeas, red onion, feta, and olives.
2. Add the dressing and stir.

**PER SERVING**
Calories: 190 | Total Fat: 7g | Protein: 10g | Carbohydrates: 22g | Sugars: 8g | Fiber: 6g | Sodium: 477mg

## Sautéed Mixed Vegetables

**Prep time: 20 minutes | Cook time: 8 minutes | Serves 4**

- 2 teaspoons extra-virgin olive oil
- 2 carrots, peeled and sliced
- 4 cups broccoli florets
- 4 cups cauliflower florets
- 1 red bell pepper, seeded and cut into long strips
- 1 cup green beans, trimmed
- sea salt
- freshly ground black pepper

1. Place a large skillet over medium heat and add the olive oil.
2. Sauté the carrots, broccoli, and cauliflower until tender-crisp, about 6 minutes.
3. Add the bell pepper and green beans, and sauté 2 minutes more.
4. Season with salt and pepper, and serve.

### PER SERVING
Calories: 106 | Total Fat: 3g | Cholesterol: 0mg | Sodium: 142mg | Total Carbohydrates: 18g | Sugar: 7g | Fiber: 7g | Protein: 6g

## Grilled Tofu and Veggie Skewers

**Prep time: 15 minutes | Cook time: 15 minutes | Serves 6**

- 1 block tofu
- 2 small zucchini, sliced
- 1 red bell pepper, cut into 1-inch cubes
- 2 cups cherry tomatoes
- 3 teaspoons barbecue sauce
- 2 teaspoons sesame seeds
- Salt and ground black pepper, to taste
- Nonstick cooking spray

1. Press tofu to extract liquid, for about half an hour. Then, cut tofu into cubes and marinate in soy sauce for at least 15 minutes.
2. Heat the grill to medium-high heat. Spray the grill rack with cooking spray.
3. Grill for 2 to 3 minutes per side until vegetables start to soften, and tofu is golden brown.
4. Serve garnished with sesame seeds.

### PER SERVING
Calories: 65 | Fat: 2.0g | Protein: 5.1g | Carbs: 10.1g | Fiber: 3.0g | Sugar: 6.0g | Sodium: 237mg

## Roasted Delicata Squash

**Prep time: 10 minutes | Cook time: 20 minutes | Serves 4**

- 1 (1- to 1½-pound) delicata squash, halved, seeded, cut into ½-inch-thick strips
- 1 tablespoon extra-virgin olive oil
- ½ teaspoon dried thyme
- ¼ teaspoon salt
- ¼ teaspoon freshly ground black pepper

1. Preheat the oven to 400°F. Line a baking sheet with parchment paper.
2. In a large mixing bowl, toss the squash strips with the olive oil, thyme, salt, and pepper. Arrange on the prepared baking sheet in a single layer.
3. Roast for 10 minutes, flip, and continue to roast for 10 more minutes until tender and lightly browned.

**PER SERVING**

Calories: 79 | Total Fat: 4g | Protein: 1g | Carbohydrates: 12g | Sugars: 3g | Fiber: 2g | Sodium: 123mg

## Zucchini Fritters

**Prep time: 40 minutes| Cook time: 10 minutes| Serves 4**

- 3 zucchinis, grated
- 2 eggs
- ¾ cups feta cheese, crumbled
- ¼ cup fresh dill, chopped
- ½ cup flour
- oil for frying

1. Place zucchini in a large colander and sprinkle with the salt.Place the zucchini between paper towels and squeeze again. Place in large bowl and let dry.
2. Melt margarine in a large skillet over med-high heat.Add to zucchini along with the feta and dill and mix well.
3. Serve with Garlic Dipping Sauce, (chapter 16), or sauce of your choice.

**PER SERVING:**

Calories: 253 |Total Carbs: 21g |Net Carbs: 18g |Protein: 10g |Fat: 15g |Sugar: 5g |Fiber: 3g

## Pita Stuffed with Tabbouleh

**Prep time: 20 minutes | Cook time: 0 minutes | Serves 4**

- 1 cup cooked bulgur wheat
- 1 English cucumber, finely chopped
- 1 yellow bell pepper, deseeded and finely chopped
- 2 cups halved cherry tomatoes
- 2 scallions, white and green parts, finely chopped
- 2 tablespoons extra-virgin olive oil
- Salt and freshly ground black pepper, to taste
- 4 whole-wheat pitas, cut in half

1. Combine the bulgur wheat, cucumber, bell pepper, tomatoes, parsley, scallions in a large bowl and stir to mix well. Season with salt and pepper to taste.
2. Place the pita halves on a clean work surface. Evenly divide the bulgur mixture among pita halves and serve immediately.

**PER SERVING**

Calories: 245 | Fat: 8.2g | Protein: 7.2g | Carbs: 39.2g | Fiber: 6.2g | Sugar: 4.2g | Sodium: 166mg

## Chickpea Coconut Curry

**Prep time: 5 minutes | Cook time: 15 minutes | Serves 4**

- 3 cups fresh or frozen cauliflower florets
- 2 cups unsweetened almond milk
- 1 (15-ounce) can coconut milk
- 1 (15-ounce) can low-sodium chickpeas, drained and rinsed
- 1 tablespoon curry powder
- ⅛ teaspoon onion powder
- ¼ teaspoon salt

1. In a large stockpot, combine the cauliflower, almond milk, coconut milk, chickpeas, curry, ginger, garlic powder, and onion powder. Stir and cover.
2. Cook over medium-high heat for 10 minutes.
3. Reduce the heat to low, stir, and cook for 5 minutes more, uncovered. Season with up to ¼ teaspoon salt.

**PER SERVING**

Calories: 410 | Total Fat: 30g | Protein: 10g | Carbohydrates: 30g | Sugars: 6g | Fiber: 9g | Sodium: 118mg`

# Chapter 8

## Soup & Stew Extravaganza

## Slow Cooker Chicken and Vegetable Soup

**Prep time: 10 minutes | Cook time: 4 hours | Serves 4**

- 1 medium potato, peeled and chopped into 1-inch pieces
- 3 celery stalks, chopped into 1-inch pieces
- 2 cups chopped baby carrots
- 2 cups low-sodium chicken broth
- 2 tablespoons tomato paste
- 2 tablespoons Italian seasoning
- 1 pound boneless, skinless chicken breasts, chopped
- Freshly ground black pepper

1. Put the potato, celery, carrots, onion, green beans, broth, tomato paste, Italian seasoning, and chicken into a slow cooker and cook on high for 4 hours.
2. Season with freshly ground black pepper.

**PER SERVING**

Calories: 232 | Total Fat: 3g | Protein: 30g | Carbohydrates: 25g | Sugars: 7g | Fiber: 6g | Sodium: 180mg

## Bacon & Cabbage Soup

**Prep time: 15 minutes| Cook time: 6 hours| Serves 6**

- 6 bacon strips, cut into 1-inch pieces
- 3 cup cauliflower, separated into florets
- 2 cup cabbage, sliced thin
- 2 celery stalks, peeled and diced
- 1 carrot, peeled and diced
- 5 cup low sodium chicken broth
- 2 cloves garlic, diced fine

1. Cook bacon in a large skillet over med-high heat until almost crisp. Remove from skillet and place on paper towels to drain.
2. Add the celery, garlic, and onion to the skillet and cook, stirring frequently, about 5 minutes. Use a slotted spoon to transfer to the crock pot.
3. Add the cauliflower and cook until tender, about 1-2 hours. Serve.

**PER SERVING:**

Calories 148 Total Carbs 8g Net Carbs 5g Protein 10g Fat 8g Sugar 3g Fiber 3g

## Black Beans Chicken Stew

**Prep time: 10 minutes | Cook time: 30 minutes | Serves 4**

- 1 tablespoon vegetable oil
- 4 boneless chicken breast halves
- 1 (10 oz.) can tomatoes with chile peppers, diced
- 1 (15 oz.) can black beans, rinsed
- 1 (8.75 oz.) can kernel corn, drained
- 1 pinch ground cumin

1. In a suitable skillet, heat oil over medium-high heat.
2. Brown chicken breasts on both sides.
3. Add tomatoes with green chile peppers, beans and corn.
4. Reduce heat and let simmer for almost 25 to 30 minutes or until chicken is cooked through and juices run clear.
5. Add a dash of cumin and serve.

### PER SERVING
Calories: 310; Fat 6g | Total Carbs: 28g | Net Carbs: 2g | Protein: 35g | Fiber: 3g | Sugars: 6g

## Turkey Cabbage Soup

**Prep time: 15 minutes | Cook time: 30 minutes | Serves 4**

- 1 tablespoon extra-virgin olive oil
- 4 cups finely shredded green cabbage
- 8 cups chicken or turkey broth
- 1 cup chopped cooked turkey
- freshly ground black pepper

1. Place a large saucepan over medium-high heat and add the olive oil..
2. Add the cabbage and sweet potato.
3. Stir in the chicken broth and bay leaves and bring the soup to a boil.
4. Add the turkey and thyme and simmer until the turkey is heated through, about 4 minutes.
5. Remove the bay leaves and season the soup with salt and pepper.

### PER SERVING
Calories: 325 | Total Fat: 11g | Cholesterol: 41mg | Sodium: 715mg | Total Carbohydrates: 30g | Sugar: 13g | Fiber: 4g | Protein: 24g

## Brunswick Stew

**Prep time: 15 minutes | Cook time: 60 minutes | Serves 6**

- 5 cups chicken broth or store-bought low-sodium chicken broth, divided
- 2 garlic cloves, minced
- 4 boneless, skinless chicken thighs
- 1 zucchini, cut into 1-inch chunks
- 1 cup barbecue sauce
- 1 tablespoon Worcestershire sauce
- ½ teaspoon not old bay seasoning

1. Select the Sauté setting on an electric pressure cooker, or until the onion and garlic are translucent.
2. Change to the Manual/Pressure Cook setting, and cook for 1 hour at high pressure.
3. Once cooking is complete, quick-release the pressure. Carefully remove the lid, and serve.

**PER SERVING:**

Calories: 262 | Total Fat: 4g | Cholesterol: 63mg | Sodium: 251mg | Total Carbohydrates: 36g | Sugar: 8g | Fiber: 5g | Protein: 22g

## Cheesy Ham & Broccoli Soup

**Prep time: 10 minutes| cook time: 6 hours| serves 8**

- 2 cup broccoli florets
- 2 cup cheddar cheese, grated
- 1 ½ cup ham, cut into small cubes
- 2 stalks celery, peeled and diced
- 1 onion, diced
- 8 cup low sodium vegetable broth
- 1/8 tsp black pepper

1. Heat the oil in a medium skillet over med-high heat.stirring frequently, about 5 minutes.
2. Add the broth, ham, celery mixture, and seasonings to a crock pot. Cover and cook on low 3-4 hours.
3. Add the broccoli and cook another 1-2 hours or until broccoli starts to get tender. Stir in cheese and cook until completely melted. Discard bay leaf and serve.

**PER SERVING:**

Calories: 214 |Total Carbs: 8g |Net Carbs: 7g |Protein: 12g |Fat: 15g |Sugar: 2g |Fiber: 1g

## Curried Carrot Soup

**Prep time: 10 minutes | Cook time: 5 minutes | Serves 6**

- 1 tablespoon extra-virgin olive oil
- 1 small onion, coarsely chopped
- 2 celery stalks, coarsely chopped
- 1½ teaspoons curry powder
- 1 teaspoon minced fresh ginger
- 6 medium carrots, roughly chopped
- 4 cups low-sodium vegetable broth
- 1 cup canned coconut milk
- 1 tablespoon chopped fresh cilantro

1. Heat an Instant Pot to high and add the olive oil.
2. In a blender jar, carefully purée the soup in batches and transfer back to the pot.
3. Stir in the coconut milk and pepper, and heat through. Top with the cilantro and serve.

### PER SERVING

Calories: 145 | Total Fat: 11g | Protein: 2g | Carbohydrates: 13g | Sugars: 4g | Fiber: 3g | Sodium: 238mg

## Tuscan Sausage Soup

**Prep time: 15 minutes| Cook time: 15 minutes| Serves 8**

- 1 lb. pork sausage, cooked
- 2 cup half-n-half
- 1 ½ cup cauliflower, grated and cooked
- ½ cup onion, diced
- ¼ cup margarine
- 1 cup chicken broth
- 4 cloves garlic, diced fine
- ½ tsp black pepper

1. In a large saucepan, over medium heat, melt margarine. Add onion and garlic, cook, stirring occasionally, 1-2 minutes.
2. Pour in the broth and cream. Bring to a boil stirring constantly.
3. Add sausage and cauliflower and season with salt and pepper. Heat through and serve.

### PER SERVING:

Calories: 336 |Total Carbs: 5g |Net Carbs: 4g |Protein: 14g |Fat: 29g |Sugar: 1g |Fiber: 1g

## Italian Vegetable Soup

**Prep time: 10 minutes | Cook time: 30 minutes | Serves 5**

- 8 cups vegetable broth
- 2 tablespoons olive oil
- 1 tablespoon Italian seasoning
- 1 onion, large and diced
- 2 bay leaves, dried
- 2 bell pepper, large and diced
- sea salt and black pepper, to taste
- 4 garlic cloves, minced
- 28 oz. tomatoes, diced
- 1 cauliflower head, medium into florets
- 2 cups green beans, chopped

1. Set a Dutch oven with oil over medium heat.
2. Mix until everything comes together. Bring the mixture to a boil. Lower the heat and cook for further 20 minutes or until the vegetables have softened. Serve hot.

**PER SERVING**

Calories: 79; Fat 2g | Total Carbs: 8g | Net Carbs: 2g | Protein: 2g | Sugar: 1g | Fiber: 2g

## Red Lentil Soup

**Prep time: 10 minutes | Cook time: 55 minutes | Serves 8**

- 1 teaspoon extra-virgin olive oil
- 1 sweet onion, chopped
- 1 tablespoon minced garlic
- 4 celery stalks, with the greens, chopped
- 3 carrots, peeled and diced
- 3 cups red lentils, picked over
- 4 cups low-sodium vegetable broth
- freshly ground black pepper

1. Place a large stockpot on medium-high heat and add the oil.
2. Add the lentils, broth, water, and bay leaves, and bring the soup to a boil.
3. Reduce the heat to low and simmer and the soup is thick, about 45 minutes.
4. Remove the bay leaves and stir in the thyme.
5. Season with salt and pepper and serve.

**PER SERVING**

Calories: 284 | Total Fat: 2g | Cholesterol: 0mg | Sodium: 419mg | Total Carbohydrates: 47g | Sugar: 4g | Fiber: 24g | Protein: 20g

## South American Fish Stew

**Prep time: 10 minutes| Cook time: 25 minutes|**
**Serves 6**

- 2 lbs. tilapia fillets, cut into bite-sized pieces
- 3 bell peppers, cut into 2-inch strips
- 1 large onion, diced
- 4 tbsp. fresh lime juice
- 14 oz. can tomato, diced and drained
- 14 oz. can coconut milk
- 3-4 cloves garlic, diced fine
- 1 ½ tsp pepper

1. In a large bowl combine lime juice, cumin, paprika, garlic, salt and pepper. Add fish and stir to coat. Cover and refrigerate at least 20 minutes, or overnight.
2. Heat oil in a large sauce pot over medhigh heat.fish and stir to combine. Add coconut milk and stir in.
3. Reduce heat to low, cover, and cook 20 minutes.Stir in the cilantro for the last 5 minutes of cooking time. Serve.

**PER SERVING:**
Calories: 347 |Total Carbs: 15g |Net Carbs: 12g |Protein: 31g |Fat: 19g |Sugar: 8g |Fiber: 3g

## Hearty Bell Pepper Stew

**Prep time: 20 minutes| Cook time: 4 hours|**
**Serves 8**

- 1 lb. hot Italian sausage
- 1 lb. lean ground sirloin
- 3 ½ cup tomatoes, diced
- 3 cup onion, diced
- 1 cup cauliflower, grated
- 4 cup low sodium beef broth
- 4 cloves garlic, diced fine
- ½ tsp oregano

1. Heat the oil in a large skillet over medhigh heat. Add in both kinds of meat and cook, place in crock pot.
2. Add the green pepper, onion and garlic to the skillet. Cook, stirring frequently, about 5 minutes.
3. Add in the broth, tomatoes, tomato sauce and seasonings. Cover and cook on high 2-3 hours.
4. Add the cauliflower and cook another 60 minutes or until cauliflower is tender.

**PER SERVING:**
Calories: 312 |Total Carbs: 14g |Net Carbs: 11g |Protein: 19g |Fat: 20g |Sugar: 8g |Fiber: 3g

# Chapter 9

## Grains, Legumes, and Pasta Assortments

## Slippery Herbed Dumplings

**Prep time: 20 minutes | Cook time: 15 minutes | Serves 8 to 10**

- 4 cups water
- 4 cups vegetable broth or store-bought low-sodium vegetable broth
- 1 cup gluten-free all-purpose flour
- 2 teaspoons baking powder
- 1 cup fat-free milk
- 2 tablespoons bottled chimichurri or sofrito

1. In a large pot, bring the water and the broth to a slow boil over medium-high heat.
2. In a large mixing bowl, all-purpose flour, baking powder, and salt together.
3. Carefully drop the dumplings one at a time into the boiling liquid.it should come out clean.
4. Serve with a small amount of cooking liquid and Smothered Dijon Chicken.

### PER SERVING:

Calories: 132 | Total Fat: 1g | Cholesterol: 1mg | Sodium: 327mg | Total Carbohydrates: 26g | Sugar: 2g | Fiber: 3g | Protein: 4

## Simple Buckwheat Porridge

**Prep time: 5 minutes | Cook time: 40 minutes | Serves 4**

- 2 cups raw buckwheat groats
- 3 cups water
- pinch sea salt
- 1 cup unsweetened almond milk

1. Put the buckwheat groats, water, and salt in a medium saucepan over medium-high heat.
2. Bring the mixture to a boil, then reduce the heat to low.
3. Cook until most of the water is absorbed, about 20 minutes. Stir in the milk and cook until very soft, about 15 minutes.
4. Serve the porridge with your favorite toppings such as chopped nuts, sliced banana, or fresh berries.

### PER SERVING

Calories: 122 | Total Fat: 1g | Cholesterol: 1mg | Sodium: 48mg | Total Carbohydrates: 22g | Sugar: 4g | Fiber: 3g | Protein: 6g

## Brussels Sprout, Avocado, and Wild Rice Bowl

**Prep time: 15 minutes | Cook time: 15 minutes | Serves 4**

- 2 cups sliced Brussels sprouts
- 2 teaspoons extra-virgin olive oil, plus 2 tablespoons
- 1 teaspoon Dijon mustard
- ¼ teaspoon freshly ground black pepper
- 1 cup cooked wild rice
- 1 avocado, sliced

1. Preheat the oven to 400°F. Line a baking sheet with parchment paper.
2. In a medium bowl, toss the Brussels sprouts with 2 teaspoons of olive oil.
3. In a small bowl, mix the remaining.
4. In a large bowl, toss the cooked wild rice, radishes, and roasted Brussels sprouts. Drizzle the dressing over the salad and toss.
5. Divide among 4 bowls and top with avocado slices.

**PER SERVING**

Calories: 178 | Total Fat: 11g | Protein: 2g | Carbohydrates: 18g | Sugars: 2g | Fiber: 5g | Sodium: 299mg

## Barley Squash Risotto

**Prep time: 10 minutes | Cook time: 15 minutes | Serves 6**

- 1 teaspoon extra-virgin olive oil
- ½ sweet onion, finely chopped
- 1 teaspoon minced garlic
- 2 cups cooked butternut squash, cut into ½-inch cubes
- 2 tablespoons chopped pistachios
- 1 tablespoon chopped fresh thyme
- sea salt

1. Place a large skillet over medium heat and add the oil.
2. Sauté the onion and garlic until softened and translucent, about 3 minutes.
3. Add the barley and kale, and stir until the grains are heated through and the greens are wilted, about 7 minutes.
4. Stir in the squash, pistachios, and thyme.
5. Cook until the dish is hot, about 4 minutes, and season with salt.

**PER SERVING**

Calories: 159 | Total Fat: 2g | Cholesterol: 0mg | Sodium: 62mg | Total Carbohydrates: 32g | Sugar: 2g | Fiber: 7g | Protein: 5g

## Butternut Noodles with Mushroom Sauce

**Prep time: 10 minutes | Cook time: 15 minutes | Serves 4**

- ¼ cup extra-virgin olive oil
- ½ red onion, finely chopped
- 1 pound (454 g) cremini mushrooms, sliced
- 1 teaspoon dried thyme
- Pinch red pepper flakes
- 4 cups butternut noodles
- 4 ounces (113 g) Parmesan cheese, grated (optional)

1. Heat the olive oil in a large skillet over medium-high heat until shimmering.
2. Fold in the wine and red pepper flakes and whisk to combine.
3. Add the butternut noodles to the skillet. cooking for 5 minutes, stirring occasionally, or until the noodles are softened.
4. Divide the mixture among four bowls. Sprinkle the grated Parmesan cheese on top, if desired.

**PER SERVING**

Calories: 243 | Fat: 14.2g | Protein: 3.7g | Carbs: 21.9g | Fiber: 4.1g | Sugar: 2.1g | Sodium: 157mg

## BBQ Chicken & Noodles

**Prep time: 10 minutes |Cook time: 25 minutes| Serves 4**

- 4 slices bacon, diced
- 1 chicken breast, boneless, skinless, cut into 1-inch pieces
- 1 cup low Fat cheddar cheese, grated
- ½ cup skim milk
- 14 ½ oz. can tomatoes, diced
- ¼ cup barbecue sauce
- homemade noodles
- salt and pepper, to taste

1. Place a large pot over med-high heat. Add bacon.Drain fat, reserving 1 tablespoon.
2. Stir in chicken and cook until browned on all sides, 3-5 minutes.
3. Stir in broth, tomatoes, milk, and seasonings. Bring to boil, cover, reduce heat and simmer 10 minutes.
4. Stir in barbecue sauce, noodle, and cheese and cook until noodles are done and cheese has melted, 2-3 minutes. Serve.

**PER SERVING:**

Calories: 331 |Total Carbs: 18g |Net Carbs: 15g |Protein: 34g |Fat: 13g |Sugar: 10g |Fiber: 3g

## Beet Greens and Black Beans

**Prep time: 10 minutes | Cook time: 20 minutes | Serves 4**

- 1 tablespoon unsalted non-hydrogenated plant-based butter
- ½ Vidalia onion, thinly sliced
- ½ cup Vegetable Broth or store-bought low-sodium vegetable broth
- 1 bunch beet greens, cut into ribbons
- 1 bunch dandelion greens, cut into ribbons
- 1 (15-ounce) can no-salt-added black beans
- freshly ground black pepper

1. In a medium skillet, melt the butter over low heat.
2. Add the onion, and sauté for 3 to 5 minutes, or until the onion is translucent.
3. Add the broth and greens.until the greens are wilted.
4. Add the black beans and cook for 3 to 5 minutes, or until the beans are tender. Season with black pepper.

**PER SERVING:**
Calories: 161 | Total Fat: 4g | Cholesterol: 0mg | Sodium: 224mg | Total Carbohydrates: 26g | Sugar: 1g | Fiber: 10g | Protein: 9g

## Healthy Loaf of Bread

**Prep time: 10 minutes| Cook time: 30 minutes| Serves 20**

- 6 eggs, separated
- 4 tbsp. butter, melted
- 1 ½ cup almond flour, sifted
- 3 tsp baking powder
- ¼ tsp cream of tartar
- 1/8 tsp salt
- Butter flavored cooking spray

1. Heat oven to 375 degrees. Spray an 8-inch loaf pan with cooking spray.
2. In a large bowl, beat egg whites and cream of tartar until soft peaks form
3. Add the yolks, 1/3 of egg whites, butter, flour, baking powder, and salt to a food processor and pulse until combined. .
4. Pour into prepared pan and bake 30 minutes, or until bread passes the toothpick test. Cool 10 minutes in the pan then invert and cool completely before slicing.

**PER SERVING:**
Calories: 81 |Total Carbs: 2g |Net Carbs: 1g |Protein: 3g |Fat: 7g |Sugar: 0g |Fiber: 1g

# Chapter 10

## Heavenly Snacks and Sweets

## Crab and Spinach Dip

**Prep time: 10 minutes | Cook time: 2 hours | Serves 10**

- 1 package frozen chopped spinach, thawed and squeezed nearly dry
- 8 ounces (227 g) reduced-fat cream cheese
- 6.5 ounces (184 g) can crabmeat, drained and shredded
- 6 ounces (170 g) jar marinated artichoke hearts, drained and diced fine
- Melba toast or whole grain crackers (optional)

1. Remove any shells or cartilage from crab.
2. Place all in a small crock pot. Cover and cook on high for 1½ to 2 hours, or until heated through and cream cheese is melted. Stir after 1 hour.
3. Serve with Melba toast or whole grain crackers. Serving size is ¼ cup.

**PER SERVING**
Calories: 105 | Fat: 8.1g | Protein: 5.0g | Carbs: 7.1g | Fiber: 1.1g | Sugar: 2.9g | Sodium: 185mg

## Cauliflower Hummus

**Prep time: 5 minutes | Cook time: 15 minutes | Serves 6**

- 3 cup cauliflower florets
- 3 tablespoons fresh lemon juice
- 5 cloves garlic, divided
- 5 tablespoons olive oil, divided
- 1½ tablespoons Tahini paste
- 1¼ teaspoons salt, divided
- Smoked paprika and extra olive oil for serving

1. In a microwave safe bowl, combine cauliflower, water, 2 tablespoons oil, garlic. Microwave on high 15 minutes, or until cauliflower is soft and darkened.
2. Transfer mixture to a food processor or blender.Add tahini paste, lemon juice, remaining garlic cloves, remaining oil, and salt. Blend until almost smooth.
3. Place the hummus in a bowl and drizzle lightly. Serve with your favorite raw vegetables.

**PER SERVING**
Calories: 108 | Fat: 10.1g | Protein: 2.1g | Carbs: 5.1g | Fiber: 2.1g | Sugar: 1.0g | Sodium: 506mg

## Crunchy Apple Fries

**Prep time: 15 minutes| Cook time: 10 minutes|**
**Serves 8**

- 3 apples, peeled, cored, and sliced into ½-inch pieces
- ¼ cup reduced fat margarine, melted
- ¼ cup quick oats
- 3 tbsp. light brown sugar
- 1 tsp cinnamon
- 1/8 tsp salt

1. Heat oven to 425 degrees. Put a wire rack on a large cookie sheet.
2. Add oats and walnuts to a food processor until the mixture resembles flour.
3. Dip apple slices in margarine, then roll in oat mixture to coat completely. Place on wire rack.
4. Bake 10 – 12 minutes or until golden brown. Let cool before serving.

**PER SERVING:**
Calories: 146 |Total Carbs: 20g |Net Carbs: 17g |Protein: 1g |Fat: 7g |Sugar: 13g |Fiber: 3g

## Chili Lime Tortilla Chips

**Prep time: 5 minutes| Cook time: 15 minutes|**
**Serves 10**

- 12 6-inch corn tortillas, cut into 8 triangles
- 3 tbsp lime juice
- 1 tsp cumin
- 1 tsp chili powder

1. Heat oven to 350 degrees.
2. Place tortilla triangles in a single layer on a large baking sheet.
3. In a small bowl stir together spices.
4. Sprinkle half the lime juice over tortillas, followed by ½ the spice mixture. Bake 7 minutes.
5. Remove from oven and turn tortillas over. Sprinkle with remaining lime juice and spices. Bake another 8 minutes or until crisp, but not brown. Serve with your favorite salsa, serving size is 10 chips.

**PER SERVING:**
Calories: 65 |Total Carbs: 14g |Net Carbs: 12g |Protein: 2g |Fat: 1g |Sugar: 0g |Fiber: 2g

## Carrot Cake Bites

**Prep time: 15 minutes | Cook time: 15 minutes | Serves 20 (1 bite each)**

- ½ cup old-fashioned oats
- 2 medium carrots, chopped
- 6 dates, pitted
- ½ cup chopped walnuts
- 2 tablespoons hemp seeds
- 2 teaspoons pure maple syrup
- ½ teaspoon ground nutmeg

1. In a blender jar, combine the oats and carrots, and process.
2. Add the dates and walnuts to the blender and process until coarsely chopped. Return the oat-carrot mixture to the blender and Process until well mixed.
3. Using your hands, shape the dough into balls about the size of a tablespoon.
4. Store in the refrigerator in an airtight container for up to 1 week.

**PER SERVING**

Calories: 68 | Total Fat: 3g | Protein: 2g | Carbohydrates: 10g | Sugars: 6g | Fiber: 2g | Sodium: 6mg

## Hoe Cakes

**Prep time: 10 minutes | Cook time: 15 minutes | Serves 16**

- 1 medium egg
- ½ cup fat-free milk
- 2 cups cornmeal
- 3 teaspoons baking powder
- 1 tablespoon unsalted non-hydrogenated plant-based butter, for greasing the pan

1. In a medium bowl, whisk the egg and milk together.
2. In a separate medium bowl, whisk the cornmeal and baking powder together.
3. Fold the dry ingredients into the wet ingredients until incorporated.
4. In a skillet, melt the butter over medium heat.
5. Add the batter in ¼-cup dollops to the spaced 1 to 2 inches apart).
6. When the edges become golden brown, turn the cakes.Repeat until no batter remains.

**PER SERVING:**

Calories: 69 | Total Fat: 2g | Cholesterol: 10mg | Sodium: 22mg | Total Carbohydrates: 13g | Sugar: 1g | Fiber: 1g | Protein: 2g

## Oatmeal Peanut Butter Bars

**Prep time: 5 minutes| Cook time: 10 minutes| Serves 10**

- ½ cup almond milk, unsweetened
- 1 cup oats
- ¼ cup agave syrup
- 6tbsp. raw peanut butter
- 2 tbsp. peanuts, chopped
- 1 tsp pure vanilla

1. Heat oven to 325 degrees. Line a cookie sheet with parchment paper.
2. Place all Ingredients, except the peanuts, into a food processor. Process until you have a sticky dough. Use your hands to mix in the peanuts.
3. Separate the dough into 10 equal balls on the prepared cookie sheet. Shape into squares or bars. Press the bars flat to ¼-inch thickness.
4. Bake 8-12 minutes, or until the tops are nicely browned. Remove from oven and cool completely. The bars will be soft at first but will stiffen as they cool.

**PER SERVING:**
Calories: 125 |Total Carbs: 14g |Net Carbs: 12g |Protein: 4g |Fat: 6g |Sugar: 1g |Fiber: 2g

## Unsweetened Chocolate Coffee Cupcakes

**Prep time: 10 minutes | Cook time: 20 minutes | Serves 24**

- 2 eggs
- ½ cup fat free sour cream
- ½ cup plant-based butter, melted
- What you'll need from store cupboard:
- 2 cup Splenda
- 1 cup almond flour, sifted
- 1 cup strong coffee, room temperature
- 4 oz. unsweetened chocolate
- ½ cup coconut flour
- 3 teaspoon of baking powder
- ½ teaspoon-salt

1. Preheat the oven to 350 degrees F. Line 12-cup muffin cups with cupcake liners. Melt the chocolate.
2. Add and beat the eggs one at a time. Stir in chocolate until well combined.
3. Pour batter into prepared cups and bake for 20-25 minutes. Let cool completely before serving.

**PER SERVING**
Calories: 173 | Total Carbs: 20g | Net Carbs: 19g | Protein: 2g | Fat: 9g | Sugar: 16g | Fiber: 1g

## Bacon-Wrapped Shrimps

**Prep time: 10 minutes | Cook time: 6 minutes | Serves 10**

- 20 shrimps, peeled and deveined
- 7 slices bacon, cut into 3 strips crosswise
- 4 leaves romaine lettuce

1. Preheat the oven to 400°F (205°C).
2. Wrap each shrimp with each bacon strip, then arrange the wrapped shrimps in a single layer on a baking sheet, seam side down.
3. Broil in the preheated oven for 6 minutes or until the bacon is well browned. Flip the shrimps halfway through the cooking time.
4. Remove the shrimps from the oven and serve on lettuce leaves.

**PER SERVING**
Calories: 70 | Fat: 4.5g | Protein: 7.0g | Carbs: 0g | Fiber: 0g | Sugar: 0g | Sodium: 150mg

## Rum Spiced Nuts

**Prep time: 5 minutes| Cook time: 10 minutes| Serves 12**

- 2 tbsp. Margarine
- 3 cups mixed nuts, unsalted
- 2 tbsp. dark rum
- 2 tbsp. Splenda
- 1 tsp cumin

1. Place a medium, nonstick, skillet over medium heat. Add nuts and cook, about 3-5 minutes, to lightly toast them.
2. Add the margarine and rum and cook.
3. Combine the remaining Ingredients in a large bowl. Add the nuts and toss to coat.
4. Dump out onto a large baking sheet to cool. Store in an airtight container. Serving size is ¼ cup.

**PER SERVING:**
Calories: 254 |Total Carbs: 10g |Net Carbs: 8g |Protein: 6g |Fat: 22g |Sugar: 4g |Fiber: 2g

# Appendix 1 Measurement Conversion Chart

### Volume Equivalents (Dry)

| US STANDARD | METRIC (APPROXIMATE) |
|---|---|
| 1/8 teaspoon | 0.5 mL |
| 1/4 teaspoon | 1 mL |
| 1/2 teaspoon | 2 mL |
| 3/4 teaspoon | 4 mL |
| 1 teaspoon | 5 mL |
| 1 tablespoon | 15 mL |
| 1/4 cup | 59 mL |
| 1/2 cup | 118 mL |
| 3/4 cup | 177 mL |
| 1 cup | 235 mL |
| 2 cups | 475 mL |
| 3 cups | 700 mL |
| 4 cups | 1 L |

### Volume Equivalents (Liquid)

| US STANDARD | US STANDARD (OUNCES) | METRIC (AP-PROXIMATE) |
|---|---|---|
| 2 tablespoons | 1 fl.oz. | 30 mL |
| 1/4 cup | 2 fl.oz. | 60 mL |
| 1/2 cup | 4 fl.oz. | 120 mL |
| 1 cup | 8 fl.oz. | 240 mL |
| 1 1/2 cup | 12 fl.oz. | 355 mL |
| 2 cups or 1 pint | 16 fl.oz. | 475 mL |
| 4 cups or 1 quart | 32 fl.oz. | 1 L |
| 1 gallon | 128 fl.oz. | 4 L |

### Temperatures Equivalents

| FAHRENHEIT(F) | CELSIUS(C) APPROXIMATE |
|---|---|
| 225 °F | 107 °C |
| 250 °F | 120 ° °C |
| 275 °F | 135 °C |
| 300 °F | 150 °C |
| 325 °F | 160 °C |
| 350 °F | 180 °C |
| 375 °F | 190 °C |
| 400 °F | 205 °C |
| 425 °F | 220 °C |
| 450 °F | 235 °C |
| 475 °F | 245 °C |
| 500 °F | 260 °C |

### Weight Equivalents

| US STANDARD | METRIC (APPROXIMATE) |
|---|---|
| 1 ounce | 28 g |
| 2 ounces | 57 g |
| 5 ounces | 142 g |
| 10 ounces | 284 g |
| 15 ounces | 425 g |
| 16 ounces (1 pound) | 455 g |
| 1.5 pounds | 680 g |
| 2 pounds | 907 g |

# Appendix 2 The Dirty Dozen and Clean Fifteen

The Environmental Working Group (EWG) is a nonprofit, nonpartisan organization dedicated to protecting human health and the environment Its mission is to empower people to live healthier lives in a healthier environment. This organization publishes an annual list of the twelve kinds of produce, in sequence, that have the highest amount of pesticide residue-the Dirty Dozen-as well as a list of the fifteen kinds ofproduce that have the least amount of pesticide residue-the Clean Fifteen.

## THE DIRTY DOZEN

The 2016 Dirty Dozen includes the following produce. These are considered among the year's most important produce to buy organic:

| | |
|---|---|
| Strawberries | Spinach |
| Apples | Tomatoes |
| Nectarines | Bell peppers |
| Peaches | Cherry tomatoes |
| Celery | Cucumbers |
| Grapes | Kale/collard greens |
| Cherries | Hot peppers |

The Dirty Dozen list contains two additional itemskale/collard greens and hot peppers-because they tend to contain trace levels of highly hazardous pesticides.

## THE CLEAN FIFTEEN

The least critical to buy organically are the Clean Fifteen list. The following are on the 2016 list:

| | |
|---|---|
| Avocados | Papayas |
| Corn | Kiw |
| Pineapples | Eggplant |
| Cabbage | Honeydew |
| Sweet peas | Grapefruit |
| Onions | Cantaloupe |
| Asparagus | Cauliflower |
| Mangos | |

Some of the sweet corn sold in the United States are made from genetically engineered (GE) seedstock. Buy organic varieties of these crops to avoid GE produce.

# Appendix 3 Index

Eugenia J. Cox

Printed in Great Britain
by Amazon

43614476R00044